AFTER SILENCE
Selected Poems of Sister Maura Eichner, S.S.N.D.

For Sister Maura's S.S.N.D. community,
family, students and friends

ACKNOWLEDGEMENTS

The poems in this book were selected and arranged by Jane Krause DeMouy, Sister Mary Ellen Dougherty, S.S.N.D., Josephine Trueschler, and Michael Storey, editor. All were longtime colleagues and friends of Sister Maura. Jane, Sister Mary Ellen, and Jo also studied under Sister Maura. Meg Storey typed the poems and assisted in copy editing. Phyllis Brill, communications director for S.S.N.D.'s Atlantic-Midwest Province, assisted with proofreading. Christine Langr, director of marketing at Notre Dame of Maryland University, provided valuable advice and assistance for the production of the book. Stephanie Coustenis of the marketing department did the book layout and designed the jacket. Kevin Raines, professor of art and longtime colleague of Sister Maura, painted Beaver Meadow Falls, reproduced on the jacket. Debbie Calhoun of the business department, who owns the painting, kindly gave permission for the reproduction. The School Sisters of Notre Dame, who own the copyrights to Sister Maura's poems, graciously granted permission for the publication of the poems in this selection. Notre Dame of Maryland University initiated and financially supported the endeavor.

AFTER SILENCE

CONTENTS

INTRODUCTION

After Silence: Selected Poems of Sister Maura Eichner, S.S.N.D.
illustrates the integration of three major disciplines in Maura's life:
School Sister of Notre Dame, poet and teacher. Maura taught as
a poet and wrote as a teacher. And she did both always within the
larger framework of her vocation as School Sister of Notre Dame.

Sister Maura Eichner was born in Brooklyn, N.Y., on May 5,
1915. When she entered the Congregation of the School Sisters
of Notre Dame in 1933 she hoped to dedicate her life to teaching
young children, preferably the poor. By 1943, however, she was
assigned to teach in the English Department at College of Notre
Dame of Maryland. She continued there with outstanding success
until 1992. Between 1945 and 1989, she published 10 books of
poetry, including *Initiate the Heart, The Word Is Love, Walking on
Water, What We Women Know* and *Hope Is a Blind Bard.* Her poems
were published in many literary magazines and journals, including
Lyric, America, Yale Review and *Commonweal;* she also published
numerous newspaper and journal articles.

A School Sister of Notre Dame for more than 75 years, Maura
lived nearly half that history in a relatively fixed, pre-Vatican II
culture, and the remaining years in a rapidly changing culture of
religious life that demanded vision, faith and flexibility. In pre-
Vatican religious life, where routine and rule prevailed, Maura
lived a rich and creative life as well as a highly relational life
within the Notre Dame community. When Vatican II eased the
constraints that canon law and custom had for years imposed on
religious communities, Maura found a rhythm and routine within
that freedom. The poems drawn directly from religious life and her
sisters in community reflect and transcend both pre-Vatican II and
post-Vatican II cultures.

Maura taught with grace and intensity. Over the years she won
several teaching awards, both local and national, including the
prestigious Theodore M. Hesburgh Award for outstanding
contributions to Catholic higher education. In her poem "A Short
History of the Teaching Profession," written perhaps for one of
her own teachers, she says: "All those words that fountained /

from her have gathered into streams / that fountain other streams / forever." Maura's teaching, too, is a testament to this kind of "gathering." In 21 years of *Atlantic* magazine student writing contests, Notre Dame students, inspired by Maura, won an astonishing 297 awards, including nine first-place awards. Her students continue her legacy in their writing and publishing as well as in their teaching.

The diversity of poetic form and the scope of subject matter gathered here demonstrate both the complexity and simplicity of her work. In form, they range from simple couplets and quatrains to the villanelle and sestina, from metered verse to free verse. Moving from Euripides to Samuel Beckett, from Augustine to an anonymous rabbi at a bus stop, from an old nun in chapel to a monastery dog, the subject matter reflects her range as a reader as well as her capacity to be present to the moment. The body of her work suggests her profound intuition and intelligence as poet and person. The force of the poetry is lodged in the power of her hope, belief and wonder at the human spirit and God at work in the human spirit. This is vintage Maura.

Maura was a poem in motion. Her presence intimated the transcendental, even when the conversation was about the mundane. Her voice, strong, steady, yet gentle, communicated a quiet authority. Graceful and articulate, always with the precise image and phrase to clarify a point, she was quiet and spectacular at the same time. Students were universally stilled by her well-crafted lectures. As a poem draws its central image to the quiet impact of conclusion, Maura ended her classes exactly on time, leaving her students knowing there was nothing more to be said. Her classes, like her person, induced the great silence.

As a teacher and as a poet, Maura was a believer. She believed in beauty—in art, in nature, in music, in painting, in language. Maura believed in life and she believed in people. Maura above all believed simply and deeply in a God who believed in beauty, and in life, and in people. In one of her later notebooks, Maura wrote, "One writes poetry in order to find God." One may well read Maura's poetry for the same reason.

Mary Ellen Dougherty, S.S.N.D.

I

WE WALK IN MIRACLES

We walk in miracles as children scruff
through daisy fields, their dresses appliquéd
with shifting tide of blossom, welkin-stuff,
the Father's white creative laughter made.

Common as spring, as bread, as sleep, as salt,
the daisies grow. Our Father made them reel
against us like the morning stars that vault
the greater home His love will yet reveal.

The petals push against the ankles, knees,
the thigh, the hands; gold pollen sifts within
the pores to rivulets of veins, to seas
of subtle life behind unsubtle skin.

O deeper and deeper than daisy fields, we drown
in miracles, in God, our Seed, our Crown.

ABRAHAM BEGAT

Going down to Canaan with his caravan,
Abram was a patriarchal sheik
as the Arabs judged. But he was the one
Yahweh called. The strong are meek.

Out of a sterile woman, he would be
Abraham, the father of a multitude.
Stars would remind him of his posterity.
Once in the evening, three men sued

for hospitality at his tent. Abraham prayed
to One. Sara, sheltered by the tent flap,
laughed at the promise, a child from their bed.
But when Isaac was born the eloquent map

of the milky way spoke genealogy. Yet Abraham
heard the command: *Take thy son
to sacrifice.* No glorias of Bethlehem
fulfilled his faith. What he won

on that mountaintop, he carried to the cave
for death. Sara had often been a shrew;
men had fought him; he could not save
Sodom; much he had wished to do

was left undone. Abraham was not
untroubled, he merely believed;
he was not impeccable, not ideal, but—
a father. We, the begotten, are not deceived.

DIALOGUE AT MIDNIGHT:
ELIZABETH TO JOHN

My son, from the chalk
hills of this old flesh
how you have sailed
beyond the waters of
your father's doubt.

I feel the small skiff
of your body. Yesterday
you leaped (rapids or
waterfall) when young
Mary walked into my arms.

What we women know.
And how much we keep
within the heart, secret
as the honeycomb that is
your skull growing in me.

My son John, trust this
first solitude. Here in the
ancient cave of my body,
sail inland water
safe from followers,

kings and dancing girls.

FROM A WOMAN'S LIFE

What Mary knew was just
enough for the usual day:
pull water, flint fire, bake
bread, smile, pray

the dark orations, sleep, wake,
wait. When pain honed a nerve,
when birth or dying clotted
an hour, she leaned to the curve

of living, resilient to fear,
laughter, suffering.
Partings are a little death.
Each one's journey is a thing

wholly without precedent.
She looked at the sky
for compass. None. She, too,
created a road to travel by.

BORN OF MARY

God's words threaded her ear bones,
intricate as a folktale journey,
God's word in fetus—alive
in her womb. Everything made him:
soil her sandals slapped, water,
mix of sunlight, dusk, strength, fear,

honey, fish, bread, memories. Fear
and desire interlock in women whose bones
are supple with life. Even well-water
Mary looked into held the nine month journey
he was making. Everything verified him.
The wholeness of her brought him alive.

He came. Helpless. Small collarbone alive
as his eyes. O his hunger. His fear—
how she felt it. When she nursed him,
the pull and suck of his mouth, the tiny bones
of maleness astonished her prayer. His journey
into time—absurd, boyish—held off the water

of a red sea from her passage. Other water,
wakening as dawn, called muteness alive
in its blessing. The twelfth year: a journey
she made with him. In Jerusalem, her fear,
intuition, epiphany among black-lettered bones
of ancient script promised her for him

that *his* bones would rise. Broken, rise. In him,
prophecy would melt all rotting ice to water,
water release hosanna-song, song be wishbones
of man's desire. That was promised. But, alive
and tossed as cattail or bulrush, fear
and faith wrestled—circling her journey.

Thirty years—not much of a journey.
Thirty to thirty-three—lifetime to him.
And to her—a following. She swallowed fear
like wayside dust. Drank his words like water.
And waited. And waited on him, alive
but almost ready the numbering of his bones.

Bones of mystery: she who humanly made him
life-giving as water, gives him to us forever alive:
balm for fear, healing way for the journey.

OUT OF CANA

John 2:1–11

The messenger came. The message was love
in a marriage feast. Would she come? grace
the young with her presence? help with the song
of her service? She began to walk to Cana. Life
on the road was busy: vendors of citrus and wine,
shepherds and sheep, and later, buoyance of dance

as the guests came into Cana. Sun-dance
too on the feasting, and Mary with deepening song
in her heart, chatting or watching the grace
of the dancers till her son came in, a life-
magnet pulling his friends along. Tender love
exchanged with glances. Then they lifted the wine

of convivial pledges: the groom, the bride, the wine
of their offspring. Time was a flowering dance
of feasting and stomping. Only the watchful love
of Mary's friend, the bride's mother, sensed the song
diminish as wine ran low. Mary moved with grace
to a servant: "Fill the water jars." "With—?" "Life."

She smiled. "Whatever he says, do it, as though your life
hung on the words of my Jesus." He did. And a grace
went out from Jesus pouring into the water-wine
Yahweh's joy. The feast renewed. The dance
danced the miracle. The mother sang her song
again: Magnificat. And Jesus poured the Father's love

in touch, in word, in wine. Marriage-love
enwrapped the groom, the bride. With sleepy grace
guests walked home singing. One more glass of wine
the friends of Jesus said. And Jesus smiled a dance
of knowing at his mother. She held his life
as kairos-gift, parting, pain, fulfilling song.

Eat bread. Drink wine. Try to sing the song
of Christ. Live life. If you can dance, dance.
Everywhere grace awaits. Desire to love to love.

PARTING

It was the day on which
he smiled, but did not take
an order for a bench;
listened, but did not make

an answer to his friends
who talked of John, said
perhaps he was the one
men waited for. His head

bent to the earth in prayer—.
More than before? Mary knew,
yet did not know. She saw
him bless the room, new

wonder in his eyes as
he asked her blessing, laced
his sandals, clasped his cloak
and simply left the place.

Then Mary was alone:
the end began with going.
The words she'd always kept
became that deeper knowing.

THE BEGINNING

Before she looked into the well-water of
her jar, she knew what she would see: as if

she were the young betrothed of Zachary,
her hair clung softly to her temples; she

touched it where it curved her cheek. More—
she knew her throat and rounding breasts grew fair,

her body gently swelled—serenity
and womanhood were one. What she could see

herself, she knew her husband looked on, too,
with love. But he was dumb. And chastened so

by Gabriel's stern rebuff, even his hand
went numb in touching her. Elizabeth planned

nothing. She kept within. Sometimes she sang
to the son in her womb. Her cousin would bring

her everything she needed. And Mary did.
Suddenly, Elizabeth could hide

nothing. Midwives gossiped and men glanced
at the priest. But woman bloomed, child danced:

O to begin to become as human as God.

ATONAL CAROL FOR THE PRESENT MOMENT

Son of God
you took life
from a gentle girl
the Jewish wife

of Joseph. You
also wholly took
our laughter, grief,
ironies and jokes.

Take us, too,
again, again,
on this lonely planet
world of men.

Orbit our veins,
look out our eyes,
be a now
surprise! surprise!

Like that human girl
who cradled you,
Son of Man,
we need you.

OUR LADY OF THE REFUGEES

Mother who knew
what hardship shakes
a woman bundling clothes
and putting by her wheaten cakes;
Mother who urged the donkey
(making happy riot
on the straggling stones)
urged the beast to be more quiet;
Mother who heard the Child
whimper beneath the thin blue shawl,
our aching prayer cries out to you,
Mother, pray for them all.

A thousand Bethlehems
mask dark tonight,
the lamps of friendly homes
have lost their light;
pathetic heaps of poor and homely things
are laid aside; a small bird sang
where a latched door swings.
Mother whose sad Egyptian flight
preceded all of these,
guide them in faith beneath familiar stars,
Our Lady of the Refugees.

SUNDAY MORNING: MIGRANT LABOR CAMP

Urine and feces
smell the chapel
door.
　　Inside, blood
dries on the feet
of migrants. They look
up to the Lady
of Guadalupe, sing,
look down
the bone-tired
body breaking
with the heart.

Sun and dust take
the altar table.
Underneath, a cat
surveys the chapel
as though it were
a birdcage.
　　In the heat,
under the skin of
children, women and men,
Jesus waits for that cup
of cold water.

WORDS OUT OF DARKNESS

for Nelly Sachs—Nobel Prize Recipient, 1966

When the packed cattle cars
stank into Belsen and Dachau,
she fled to Sweden with

nothing left but language.
All the children whose hair
would never again need

to be brushed, all the men
whose tongues had licked up
latrine flies,

all the women whose wombs
had been filled with experiment
never left her thought.

The flesh of prophets
tore on the barbed wire
fences; wings of angels

were gnawed by hungry rats.
Solomon kept a journal in the attic
of Anne Frank.

Distance is more terrible than
presence. Horror the mind envisions
copulates with sleeplessness.
In Sweden Yahweh burned like snow.

LITANY FOR THE LIVING

Hildegard of Bingen
Catherine of Genoa
Catherine of Siena
Mechtild
Simone Weil
Edith Stein
Julian of Norwich
Teresa of Avila
Therese of Lisieux
Etty Hillesum
Marjorie Kempe
Mary Ward
our cloud
of witnesses
of flaming heart
light untouchable
dark immeasurable
mystic marriage
ground-of-being-God
the Father
God the Mother.

SLIGHT GLOSS ON REVELATIONS OF DIVINE LOVE

Juliana of Norwich, Ancress, 1342–1413

Outside Norwich
was a hazelnut tree.
For Juliana
it was a mystery

of which she said
by analogy
as God made this,
so God made me;

as He keeps and loves
the fruit of this tree,
even so He loves
and keeps me.

While Chaucer mocked
at mockery
and the Black Plague smelled
out mortality,

shrill peasants hacked
the manors down;
war dug like a tick
at the English crown;

churned up preachers
taught that men
could splice the text
with a rubric amen.

And Juliana said
of the hazelnut,
it seems but little
in peril, but

made, kept and loved,
it is wholly His:
here for certitude
is all that is.

LITTLE BALLAD FOR THE MOMENT

Down came Zaccheus,
branch to branch,
down came Zaccheus
rubbing his calf,
for he hadn't shinned
up a sycamore tree
in more than half
a century.

Down came Zaccheus
planning the meal:
delicious dishes,
herbs to smother
fresh-caught fishes,
warm baked bread,
honey and dates,
wine so red
the fine bouquet
hung in the air
like a young girl's hair.

Down came Zaccheus,
saying: "honest, I
will give it back—
not someday,

but *now*: all that
I cheated and took
by baiting or better—
with a taxman's hook
and a warning, "fail—
and I promise you jail."

Down came Zaccheus,
branch on branch
and Jesus waiting
to give him a chance
to be free.

Coda
Lord, when taxes are
heavy and due (always)
so it seems right now,
and what they call
world-wide inflation
has a time span of
eternal duration,
Lord, between you and me,
call down Zaccheus
from my sycamore tree.

CHRISTMAS: THE REASON

God chose a barn where hay was sweet, where a cow
would wait familiar nudge upon her flank
till steaming spray ringed the pail, where a plough-
blade cut a shadow on the floor, old planks

half-buttressing the wall. Barley and oats
rode in granary bins under the sway
of a spider web. Mice bulged with feed. The cat
watched. A farmer's boy, smelling of hay

and silage brought lamplight to his chores.
Then dark. A young man helped a woman in.
Time unsealed her rounded womb. And meteors
struck earth-atmosphere with joyous din

of light. A newborn cried. So men keep seed
in barns—to plant a miracle at need.

THE CHILD

He created a world.
Yours. Mine. Shall we ever
explore it?

His fingers curled
on yours, mine, sever
our hold on everything

else. Will he—
live? We are uncertain,
in a dark:

a centered fluidity,
an albumen planet.
Out of your seed

in me, he *is*.
And he has made us
a people.

totally his.
We are almost ready
for God.

CHRISTMAS STAR

'Adoration of the Magi' carved on whale-
bone 12th C.: Victoria and Albert Museum

A formal veil curves about the mother's face.
Chiseled bone, the imagined cloth of gold,
falls to her crossed ankles and the bouquet
of English meadow flowers they hold.

Tall kings crowd forward, nudging
worshiping beasts that crouch along
their robes, nuzzle their walking staffs.
Her Child is God. In whale-bone song

a single daisy is the carven star:
good news in spring's vernacular.

INNERMOST

On the eve of hope, come, let us be
silent as joy, certain as change,
here before this Christmas tree.

Tassels of wind hang secretly
among berries and fruit and winter sun
that warmed the boughs of this tree.

Ghosts of butterflies delicately
shadow a branch, melt like snow
in the intimate dark of this tree.

A nest where robins were epiphany
clings to the flesh of the trunk
of this music and moon-gilded tree.

With carols and quiet let us be
reawakened to faith, purified,
giving as branches of this tree.

Circled about love's mystery,
O for a moment fulfilled in light,
we are one in a word, a tree.

LOVE TRAVELS FAR

Love travels far
to be home.
Carols echo—
"Come, O come…"

God is where
He chose to be—
living in you,
living in me.

FRIENDSHIP WITHOUT END

He walks into the shabby room
gently. This world, too, will break
like a fever from the blackening tomb

of itself. He looks at his students.
Under the look, each man is alone,
astonished at the courtesy. "Who has condemned

you?—Neither will I." He serves
his students. A chair. A book. A glass
of water. The frailty of man deserves

redemption. He speaks—only a word,
a few words. Men gather the manna of
his praise. They have not often heard

themselves so reverenced. He
listens to them. Listening is a hand
on the shoulder, strength, mystery.

He turns their hearts to flesh. Grief,
fear, shriveling, loneliness, terror
are eased in the humility of his belief.

Such is the presence of a friend.
Such a presence does not end.

From the Book of Commonplace Revelation

Uneasy afternoon:
tea-colored sky

silence waiting
for a tornado.

You and I
rode home like

women expecting
a drug field

at the turn
of the stair.

Instead—rain
piercing as nails

or bricks
facing a heart,

water hissing
like whetstone

on a knife-
grinder's wheel.

Ah—
suddenly

across housetops
and trees

the noiseless
explosion

of sun beams
in every drop

of rain
an arc

a curved
wet handle

of an anchor—
a rainbow—

mooring us
in the faithfulness

of God.

Easter Morning

We were not in a
place, though gnats
rising from wet grass

proclaimed their meadow.
We were not in a
time, though rafts of

light unmoored from the
eastern line of trees. We
were becoming, hearing

our hearts beat in a
rhythm impossibly possible:
60 trillion cells of every

human person affirming
not seeing is believing.

FOR THE NEW OCCUPANTS

The house is 80 years old.
The wood is soft-boned.
They have taken old windows
out and eased in the new
on honed aluminum frames.

Behind the glaze, you will
hear the wind thrumming
names from the past:
code on glass.

In and out of this old house
spirits move. It holds
a resonance of grief.
It is an ancient flume of love,
belief, beyond belief.

FLESH MADE WORD

It is hard,
Beckett says,
to accept the light.
"God is love.
Yes or no?
No."

And yet
this thirst
for infinity.
Nothing satisfies.
Everything falls
short.

Then,
ready or not,
this child comes,
reading his mother's eyes,
needing her breast.

But only a child,
mind you,
flesh that could
hang from a nail
from horny wood.

Why, in the night,
should we reel
from the shock
of that presence?
find in our doubt
and sweat
this astonishing hope?

WALKING ON WATER

Your ankles are jeweled with irregular wheels
of bright water; you walk on outgoing tide
like Noah's frail ark. I know what it feels

like to walk on the water from standing beside
you, telling my eyes to look through natural air,
through funneling clouds that stormily hide

the voice that upholds. I have seen that you dare
to walk on a tear, on the styx, a landlocked bay
when *come* is the classic and only answer to prayer.

On gnarled roots of water or wind bent combers of
gray, you hold up the world on a lever of spray.

II

CREATION

At four, Maura meets the tiger lilies
at the garden border, eye
to golden cup. She looks within
the heart.
And, amber, ochre, yellow cry
a soft response: come in, come in.

Maura goes. As bee to clover,
or to open rose, so she—
drawing up not pollen but a light
that flows
into herself, so bright,
that when she turns to us she glows

with wonder, and we see the old
wild flower border not just there,
a swaying floating golden aura,
but God
calling into being in the summer air
this gift for Maura.

LAST SNOW

Less alive than a Rockwell Kent scene
and more real: suburban afternoon hills
foundering in trampled snow and thin
interlocking up and down voices. Bells

of ice crystal ring from hemlock and pine
but the children do not hear.
They flop on sleds; gasp and keen
at runners blurring to spray; dare

the bounce between the hillocks; lunge
into crisp, sun-riddled banks. When dusk
clings to red soggy snow pants, and strange
six-rayed stars hang from mittens, they risk

"one more, just one more ride," before the long
pull home. Last elation fiercely cries
"tomorrow we'll come again, tomorrow we'll bring
the others." Their weighted bodies drowse

toward dreaming, while the south winds blow
rumoring the hills with morning thaw.

GUATEMALA

The cloth strap fitted across his forehead,
twisted into rope above his shoulders.
It held the homemade box
on his back. In it his son lay dead.

Mid-day enlargement of white sun
glazed the box; sweat and held back tears
polarized the father's eyes to the beaten road
from the coffee plantation to the dry dun

of the workers' cemetery. At home, the mother
wailed; the children fumbled uneasily
among chickens and rabbits, uncertain
of the life they saw in each other.

The father stood a long time at the grave
he had dug. He could not bear to lift
the strap from his brow, release the box
from his back. His wet shoulders gave

in at last. He let the coffin into the hole
carefully—as a man puts good seed in earth.

LITTLE MARTYROLOGY

There is a boy here that hath five barley
loaves, and two fishes....
John 4:9

"So you followed the preacher all through the day,
a son of mine, letting himself be led
by a man from Nazareth. You did, didn't you?"
"Yes," he said.

He looked down at the fishes—white belly
on silver back, and the brown crusts of barley bread.
Light like a cross on all of it.
"Yes," he said.

"At least you brought the basket back. They talked
of your giving the food to him instead.
Rake the fire. Clean the fishes."
"Yes," he said.

He laid the knife to head and fin.
On this food the hillside-people had been fed.
"Hurry. We waited long enough for you."
"Yes," he said.

"You think the fish will be a sign, maybe?
and there is something holy in the bread?
Get ready for the evening meal. We need the food."
"Yes," he said.

Mature and lonely, ungarrulous and wise,
the boy laid loaves upon the table, spread
open fish upon the coals. "Stop mooning. Sit. Eat."
"Yes," he said.

INTERLINEAR: ELEGY FOR A YOUNG MAN

The Mother remembered how he had cut out paper snowflakes,
the paper creased and crossed in angles less acute
than blurred. But it didn't really matter for his blunted scissors
followed pleats and cornices in polarized pursuit.

    Snow crystals smelled the air,
    though none had fallen yet.
    He decided to put the chains on the tires
    before the roads were wet.

How his childhood fingers had opened the paper crystals
on the kitchen table; how he laughed and tossed
about the locked hexagonal stars; how the winter sun
was lavish on his thick unmelting heraldry of frost.

    Between bride and groom the windshield glass
    and epithalamion-refrains.
    He pulled his happy vision down
    to lock the tires with the chains.

No ice on branches of air so perfectly assumed
as this wobbly consonance of honeycomb design;
this stenciling of snowflakes in the tame emerald sunlight,
and the boy absorbed in acquiescent miracles of line.

    The truck careened around the corner.
    They never showed his body to his bride:
    chaotic flesh and wardrobe montage,
    and, unattached, the hand neatly flung aside.

Between the child cutting crystallines from drawing paper
and the young man home from his Pacific stint
and smiling at his bride, the smell of snow was on the air,
the frost unseasonal which grey skies hint.

Now snow like an unexpected mirror-image
is cryptic petrifaction of a grief
less real than the remembered boy in sunlight
cutting snowflakes in a wonder of belief.

Teen Age Daughters at Breakfast

They have returned, the beautiful strangers
who are my daughters. I fill the white coffee cups.
Pass the cream pitcher. Out of my dream of danger
these women have come to our home. My lips
      open to speak. But I listen.

Where have they been? They sailed on the river
of summer. They balanced the hovering sun
on their breasts. Who was the taker? the giver?
They? or Apollo—bemused by my daughters, won
      from his lyre to listen.

All day on the river my daughters dallied.
The watery boards of the boat are signed
with their bodies: heart and pulse beat tallied
in mellow raft wood. Who shall I find
      in their voices? I listen.

All day. Through to dusk and to moonlight
my daughters rode on the river. When? when
the returning? I lay in the wind dune, sight-
less, unsleeping. Longed for the footsteps again.
      In the silence, I listened.

My exquisite daughters the sun god has taken
casually pass the butter, the jam, the toast.
Salt and honey, amber and sea spray waken
to glory the faces I love. I stand on the coast
      of their morning. I listen.

Duo Ecstatica

They walk—hand in hand—through the square.
The sun has brought the deck chairs out
and a tuppence of ease to lidded eyes
sleepily watching the sprayed-up hair
of the girl with the boy in the square.

They have left the playground swings and bars
years too early for this hand in hand
clamor of blood and flesh; suddenly summer denies
no one, not even the boy and the girl in the square.
His hands leap to her breasts, her hair,
his lips to her mouth and the wild kiss cries
like a discovered bird. They break apart.

In the deck chairs, under uneasy sun,
hardly a lidded eye moves, only thighs start
and stretch, one by one.

BEATNIK

There were three John the Baptists in
the gallery that afternoon. A piece
you might expect—a Renaissance
modello for an altar: Veronese'
gentle John held the ribbed shell
trickling water on the head
of Christ where radiance fell,
ruminating on mystery. Rouoult bled
John of prophecy: thick outline
of elemental man.

              No freshet, nor river wash
touched the third. He had begun
familial likeness with a beard;
had honey and locust in the espresso café
and carried *Children of the Bomb*
as primal staff.

Courtauld Galleries, London

THE SUICIDE

Though he had longed
for the calm of water
when the car climbed
Bay Bridge, he was afraid.

He felt so alone.
He was the erring son.
No one he had ever tried
to love was near.

Midway on the bridge,
motor running, he thrust
at the door and
leaped the guard rail.

He hit the water
arms outspread
like Jesus sweating
on his face

in garden grass.
No one saw
ministering angels
under water.

MARRIAGE SONG

I have come that you may have life
and have it more abundantly.

i   God speaks

Love-language is my very word
 love-language
  love
 bride and groom
is the flesh I dreamed you of.

Wine fills all my water jars
 wine fills all
  wine
 bride and groom
is my life in you, my living vine.

You are hope, you are new joy,
 you are hope
  you
 bride and groom
are my promise: I make all things new.

Be in love, my chosen ones, with life,
 be in love
  be
 bride and groom
in each other deep in love with me.

ii　*response of the bride and groom*

Our love, our Father, is in You.
　　By this encircling ring
　　　we vow fidelity.
　　Our pulse and heart beat sing
in You we live our lives abundantly.

We are the dancers, we who dance
　　in one mysterious design.
　　　We vow a mystery
　　of love: each the giver, each the sign
of reverence for the wholeness of reality.

We are the lovers You created,
　　we move in revelation
　　　gesture and word
　　discover deeper than we dreamed
a selflessness eye has not seen, nor has ear heard.

We are Your seed, O Father, and in us
　　Your seed will miracle:
　　　uniquely, we,
　　in delight and awe and ecstasy
recreate Your love in our humanity.

iii   *praise of the wedding guests*

Let harp and flute and timbrel play
     again for Cana-feasting.
          Let the Lady Mary say
          Do whatever He shall tell you…
and joy upon the bride and groom this day.

Let Christ be friend, be wedding guest today.
     Communing in the Eucharist
          we are with Him and pray
     His smile upon our festival,
His laughter on the laughter of this day.

New wines and old—vintage bouquet
     raise for the groom. And for the bride
          a roundelay
     of heart-deep blessing. Bride and groom,
we renew our love of life in you today.

Sing   amen   amen   on an alleluja day
     sing and rejoice—parents
          children   friends   all who say
     God came to bring life: here is God's life
O radiant bride, O strong, good groom. O alleluja day.

A Woman Is Waiting for a Bus

in the rain, in Baltimore.
Even her big red umbrella
is speechless about courage,
journey's end, the door

of home. Two buses (not
her transfer) pass. She stands
in flooding rain, bulky as
an ark waiting for ararat.

The third bus has come
—gone. She huddles
into rain. Wind sloshes
wetness across her numb

flesh. Open to receive
bitter weather and give back
warmth, she waits—black
ancient beautiful eve.

CELEBRATION

The blues band rhythmed
it out in the back yard
where hard-driving tunes
chopped summer air like
blades of a helicopter.
But nobody got lifted up.
The great grandchildren's
friends laughed—rump
hitting rump.

Ms. Fay in heavy white
hand crocheted lace and
heavier pearls did not jog
her cane to the beat.
Ms. Fay's dress came many
years ago from one of the
white ladies she worked
for. One of her nephews
who wrote songs gave
her the pearls.

She listened now to
politicians in her back
yard making campaign
speeches. She said
nothing. Almost she had
lived her first hundred
years in D.C. where it was
easier to get hashish than
hominy grits.

Ms. Fay had her patience
a long time. She brought it,
she said, from Brethren
Baptist Church in King's
County when she was a girl.
There were horses and cows
in the field when she came
to Union Station. She had
trust in the Lord, too.

She blew hard at the hundred
birthday candles, a little
tired. She didn't, she said,
know how many more years
with or without candles, but
what she had would last.

BACK PORCH FUNDAMENTALIST

In the afternoon
he chose the corner in the sun.
Then he set his porch rocker
facing the mimosa
where gold wires
of light tapped
the leaves, and he, himself,
by a simple act of seeing
observed a miracle.
If anything is, he said,
them pods
on this tree is the keys
of the kingdom.

ISHTAR, THE MONASTERY DOG

When the nun worked tenderly in the sun pit,
sorting the pale leaves of lettuce, thinning
radish and cress, smiling at daily miracles
of lacy spine of carrot, overlapping cabbage leaves,
Ishtar, the dog was with her.

When she walked through a fallow field—
sweet vernal grass, cocksfoot, broomcorn
and timothy clinging to her denim
apron and the moving psaltery of Benedictine robes,
Ishtar, the dog walked with her.

When she opened the monastery gate to the gift
of sheep, the new and solid plain-song of the ram,
the ewe; processionals of herding, gathering,
lambing, dipping, worming, shearing,
Ishtar, the dog guarded the sheep.

Older and older and slower and slower
the dog moved faithful to the deep seasons'
mystery, and the nun whose tall compassion
farmed the monastery land. So it was. When
Ishtar, the dog died of old age

—for days and days the thigh of
the nun was numb—was strangely sore—
like a spot on the lip of
the mouth where a trumpet hung.
Ishtar, the dog.

MIDEAST: SUMMER TOUR

They remember the driver of the bus,
a tough and gentle Jew.

Long after Tel Aviv, the Lake of Galilee,
the Jordan Valley and Jerusalem,
Bethlehem and Hebron,
when they rode down to Sinai,
braced against washed-out roads,
dieting on dust and heat,
sucking the last saliva to their lips,
before they reached a dig
and excavation shade, he never let
one of them forget the land.

He'd brake the bus: *Look:*
they saw a curving neck lift
lyre horns, a swift gazelle
leap into the dusk; long-eared sheep;
a desert falcon climb the cloudless sky;
red mountainside; granite monastic walls
where, long ago, Moses learned the law.

The driver smiled at them: *Shalom.*
Lightly he dropped his hands
to the submachine gun on his knees.

CENTRAL AMERICA: FOOTNOTE ON SOCIAL HISTORY

Peasants found the bodies of four women by a roadside in the
village of Santiago Nonualo on Dec. 3, 1980. They were identified
as Maryknoll sisters Ita Ford and Maura Clarke, Ursuline
nun Dorothy Kazel and lay worker Jean Donovan. They were
allegedly raped then shot at close range.
Newsweek, June 4, 1984

Herod ordered the killing.
Shoot them with their hands open
to give hope to the helpless.
Ita, Dorothy, Jean, Maura

It was done. Like felons,
they were hidden in unmarked graves,
scapegoats, caked with blood.
Dorothy, Jean, Maura, Ita

Later, hauled by ropes
cutting breasts, ankles, wrists, their
loose-hanging heads gaped with gun holes.
Jean, Maura, Ita, Dorothy

Ramah's voice wails and laments.
Unseen, four queenly women waken
our hearts to wonder, freedom, God.
Maura, Ita, Dorothy, Jean

LETTER FROM SANTA CRUZ

I do not know the date.
Calendars have no meaning here.
One hundred miles north (or
maybe more) from Santa Cruz
our families live or try to live
(and fail) farming rice.

Five years ago only monkeys
talked and swung in jungle trees.
There is a road, but not
when there is rain. It had been
raining long when Marta died.

Months ago, a doctor passing
through, told Marta that she ought
to get to Santa Cruz. Some time, some
time, Marta said, she would.

She was busy at the well when
the growth was big enough
to stop the last thin breath
from edging up her throat.

Sunsets in the tropics go like
that—gold, amber, scarlet—
then the dark.

That night, Felipe came, sat
in silence, said the child
must be removed from Marta's body
otherwise Marta would be too
heavy to rise up to heaven.

No one argued. What must be done
is always done. Twenty four
hours after her death, Marta
was buried with her child
born as no one living has been
born.

Think of us sometimes. We have
some medicines, and a syringe.
We have a mirror—will it
cloud with breath? We choose
a feather from the breast of some
small bird. Will it stir?

Fires burn holes in darkness
when the living wait upon
the dead.
      We push at memories
as at a willful strand of hair.
Somewhere, you are at a desk
trying to splice language to
reality.
      And I am here,
my feet wrapped in wet grass,
my hands open to receive
whoever comes.

On Having a Conference with a Student

The world is happening. And she
sits here like a pale gold ikon.

Her words are a fragment of Sappho.
I think of Van Gogh's flowering

almond spray. She is hidden as a
drop of pure water in a cup.

Into her heart suffering has come.
Pain has discovered the secret depth.

Margaret, daughter of Thomas More,
Cordelia, Alcestis, Miranda walking

in the meadow of young love, Beatrice
smiling into the choir of the stars.

From the cosmos of her heart, I hear
the alpha singing, *Be glad, Mary...*

journeying through delicate
veins to the omega of her joy.

Here is the sacrament that I receive.

SURGEON

In visible fatigue, he leans
back in the office chair,
musing the footnotes of autobiography.
On the bare

branches of his absolute skill,
memory, anecdote,
blossom like honey locust.
His grandfather wrote

Indian ballads; was a good
minister to the Cherokee.
In the evenings
he read "Antigone"

in Greek or sipped
vintage wine
in the "Aeneid." The surgeon
shrugs. The line

of his frontier is deed.
What can the supple hands
give? A little more life.
He says—weariness be damned—

and rides up from remembering
like a diver; bases
his chair; strides to
surgery; outraces

withering cells.
He chooses: dares
man's ultimate reach—
humanly to care.

JULY 4, 1863

General Lee withdrew
from Gettysburg.

Scent of full orchards
apple and peach,
smell of ripe wheat
in the valley
had fled before him.

Left on the field:
unburied boys
in heavy clay
and coolness of marsh.

Each with his
petrified life:
hand on the
Testament,
diary for Agnes,

a fishhook,
a snuffbox,
the hair of his
mother,
a pipe, a comb,
a pencil, a
letter for Anna.

Heat and air
and rain on
their bodies:
a valley of
wheatfields,
of orchards
of apple
and peach.

On the Road to Charlottesville

When they came back, with regimental cloth
hanging like rags from wasted bodies,
it was up this road they trudged.

Young master dragged a lantern he had
unhooked from a deserted stable wall.
Sancho bent under winters and a bag

of rot—all the two of them
had clawed from the bereavement
of each day.

Cutting from the road, up this walk
they came, past the sultry meadow,
the pond lined with weeds, the hollow

where a fox had been torn.
There was a bark, and the last
of the golden labradors leaped

from under a broken porch.
A candle hesitated, then took flame.
A door rattled cautiously.

Then they were in a circle of women,
faces in slow grieving motion,
planets around the candle flame.

Later, a grandson of the soldier
set up this stone: To commemorate
seventy five slaves

and especially Sancho Panza
who served his master
1861–1865.

Awakening

William is with us,
a place and a name;
they cannot remember
when he came.

William's face is soft like dusk,
his smile is blind
to mutability
and stratas of the mind.
His thick hands lift
the hydrangea mound,
nibble the sand, and weed
the mustard from the ground.
His old mop shuffles,
piling a crust
of summer pollen, winter smoke,
in parallels of dust.
All the straightness gone from him,
steps wearied away,
he is some slow angelus,
tolling out a day.

William sags
from shoulder to shoulder;
it must be I
who am growing older.

THE GRANDMOTHER

This is a daguerreotype
of the Irish grandmother
come from Wicklow
with a bit of heather

the customs officer
did not find
dried into her bundle.
Mountain rock, sand,

silence, work—these
she knew.
But here, unbelieving,
the blazing blue

eyes stare
at the black click
of the photographer.
It was like

that when she died:
lonely, open eyes
asking that Wicklow
be paradise.

STILL LIFE: WAITING

Genesis 18:1–14

The birches are composed
as a Japanese print: mourning
doves move smoothly

through untended grass
around the feeder and the stone
bird bath rooted

like a sun dial in time.

Samantha, the cat,
has wandered away, though someone
continues to fill

her bowl with water.

My brother sits in the shadow
like old Abraham, ready,
hoping that someone will come

with a message different
from the unseen chorus
singing Sophoclean tragedy.

My brother's wife,
skeletal and bald
with the crazed demands

of disease, waits,
sheathed in sheets,
for three angels to come

with promises of life,
wild impossible promises
which will make her laugh

as Sarah did.
She longs to have God
fill his cup

with her laughter.

The Father

Luke 15:11–32

Never had the old man made such a journey.
His robes enfolded him like driving wind.
No one remembered the old man running. Even fire
had never moved him. His estates were the light
of the town. Yet, there he was, running to a dark
figure huddling the road. Love was flood-water

carrying him forward. Some tried to dike the water;
nothing could hold him. Love loosed a wind
of words: "My son is coming home." Dark
grief behind, the father ran, arms open as light.
He had to lift the boy before his son's fire
of sorrow burned the father's sandals. Journey?

The old man could remember no other journey
but this homecoming: he held his son in the fire
of his arms, remembering his birth: water
and fire. Servants ran along thrusting at the wind
of excitement: what shall we do? what torchlight
prepare? "Bathe away the pig-pen-slopping-dark

that cloaks my son. Prepare a banquet. Jewel the dark
with fires. My son was dead. My son is afire
with life. The land is fruitful. Joy is its water.
Where is my eldest son? The end of the journey
is ours. My son, do you grieve? turn from the light
to say you are unrewarded? Son, is the wind

from the south closer than you to me? is the wind
of your doubt stronger than my love for you? Water
your hardness, my son. Be a brother to the dark
of your brother's sorrow. Be a season of light
to his coming home. You will make many a journey
through cities, up mountains, over abysses of fire,

but for tonight and tomorrow, my eldest, fire
your heart, strike at its stone. Let it journey
toward dawning, be a thrust at the dark
your brother will never forget. Find a woman of water
and fire, seed her with sons for my name and wind-
supple daughters for bearing daughters and sons of light.

I am a father of journeys. I remind you the dark
can be conquered by love-blazing fire. I made air and wind
a compassionate homeland. Be at home in the light."

THE GRANDMOTHER SPEAKS

In spite of myself, I sometimes thought,
amid all changes, *he* will not change:
my grandson John will be fifteen forever.
When he came to visit me, chided by
his mother into coming, he stared at me.
He was sulky, arrogant, bored, daring,

tough. I watched my grandson John daring
me to love him. What pressure, I thought,
pain, peer talk—turned him from me?
Yet when he came, burdened with change,
a small ghost slipped in, too. He stood by
my grandson John, laughing, forever

ready to run to my arms. What's forever?
Not long, really. I know that. My daring
grandson, at two, leaped for my arms. By
three, we played the world. But I thought
five and six were the best: there was a change,
but what a change—glorious. He taught me

to read again. He leaned into me
as we read: 'and so they lived forever—
happy with each other.' If sea-change
had taken him—after those days—a daring
virus lassoed him...though I thought
I could not bear it, now I know we live by

memories as well as breath. Ghost, standing by
fifteen year old John, you tease me,
call me, love me out of my darker thought.
Fifteen is not forever. You are forever.
You are my *Our Town* Emily—daring
to come back. My grandson John will change

as I change. The son of my son will change,
grow into manhood, into lover and father. By
the time his roots have deepened, daring
to find his self-hood, he may visit me
in greener fields. No matter. Forever
is ours. When I grieved and thought—

change is loss, what I lost was the me
that lives by change, but loves forever:
I dare to trust the heart of my thought.

THE BIRTH OF CHRIST: NURSING HOME

The nursing home is isled in trees:
locust, tulip, dogwood and pine,
with a harp of poplars to the north
on the crest of a hill.

At the first or second snow, white crusts
cling to bark and branch, and the sun that
melts it all to wetness, also lacquers it
with transient light.

But no pine boughs or hemlock spray are
brought indoors at Christmas time. Fire law.
Bright satin balls hang like golden apples
for this all hallowing eve.

The old ones shrink into their chairs; hang
like unsteady wrens from corridor rails.
When their eyes cloud, sometimes light
seeps under the skin.

When ears fail, finger ends listen along
the halls, or to a hand, or at a breast strong
enough to be a wailing wall, or soft enough
to be a pillow—briefly.

Who comes Christmas night to the nursing home?
The hurried and dutiful, frightened, fatigued,
the wanting to be grateful, ill at ease, loving,
and longing to be kind.

What comes Christmas night to the nursing home?
Remembrance—more alive than supple thighs
of nurses' aides, more aching than claws that grip
arthritis to the spine.

Like thick snow and moonlight glazing dogwood
boughs, memory illuminates this night.
Angels move like glorias to Bethlehem
passing high-rail beds.

Who comes? who comes? more real than night
nurses? That child, called Word, but whom
they know as *Child*. And the blood warms
one more time.

A Short History of the Teaching Profession

Fifty two years ago
when the first grade tumbled
like a gaggle of geese
into her classroom, they looked up—
startled—at the great tree
she was to shelter them.

Slowly they quieted to her
gentle intimacies of phonics,
bittersweet learning to read.

Today, one of those children
stands beside her coffin
looking down at the face
weathered with hope,
touching the hand.
Bone and flesh hardly intervene.

All those words that fountained
from her have gathered into streams
that fountain other streams
forever.

THE TOOTH POINT

After she died
no one
needed him.

He rode downtown
and returned
to no one.

He listened
to his grandchildren
speaking words

to which no dictionary
gave him clue.
Mostly he dined alone.

He never realized
how much food
was gristle.

He still wore
a chain of being
across his vest

only now
it held a time piece
which scarcely moved.

EACH DAY

Her face thins almost
as we watch. Bones

seem larger—grating
on pillow and sheet

like shells on a hedge
of shore. We speak

more simply in her presence:
a primer of nouns

and verbs. She lets go
of life gently. We

receive from her hands
the victory of belief,

learning the meaning of
our lives from our grief.

The Old Nun

Standing up or sitting down,
it is the same.
Her back is knuckled out and hunched,
her eyes have lost the flame
of seeing;
sound has crunched itself to murmurs,
that is all.

She sits in chapel
in the last dim stall
like some old hunting dog
who keeps the scent
nose-pointed, ears set
on the way his master went.

The hearth brushed,
the hound drowsing
is suddenly stirred
by the faintest rousing
sound of the horn.

The Hunter, the Hunter,
a golden cup
filled with Hunter's scarlet—
up, dog, up.

FLIGHT IN AUTUMN

"Look, oh look," I heard you call,
"the geese are going south."
We leaned upon the garden wall;
behind your tilted head
your upturned hand, I stared
into the thin shellac of sun
upon the oaks. I dared
not say I could not find the darkened wedge
against the skies.
You turned grey, guileless eyes
to me and then I saw
the flight of geese,
the pattern of the primal law.

"And did you hear," you said,
"the strange wild sound they make?"
I who stirred
one moment too late
for cry or wing
of any live thing,
I had not heard.

But I could share
the startled breath upon your words,
the gentle touch of buoyant hand
curved to ancient rite of birds;
know the sound of open feather,
the headlong cry on brittle weather:
feel autumn on my eyes and mouth;
hear and see the geese fly south.

Morning

A few oak
and sycamore
shadows
float quietly
in water.
The sun
like a master
of candlelight
pierces city haze.
Around the reservoir
the joggers
tlot tlot
through an
outcry of
gnats
tlot tlot
an exhaustion
of weeds
tlot tlot
on the mesmerizing
circle of
Poseidon's
city pond—
men
stalking
their future,
blunting
the paunch
of Bacchus.

NOVEMBER EVENING

On the barberry bush the ripe fruit hangs
in hazardous suspense of wind and cold;
the yellow of the walnut tree
is some dim memory of spattered gold.
Enough for the gum tree—a runner spent
and silent from the chase—
it leans against the oak, with all its breath
spilt out in scarlet pools about its base.
A day or two the maple will be done
with crimson noons and dusks of Chinese red;
by hours now the end of autumn slips away.
With silhouettes alone the eye is winter fed.

Tonight, ankle deep in great oak leaves,
mocha and russet, fawn and brown,
vaguely moist and stiff from somber rains,
we crush the seasoned harvest down.

Press the acorn underfoot, press the pod to earth,
knowing if this be death, this, too, is birth.

FALL OF A KINGDOM

At a banquet
to please his guests

Charlemagne served
one thousand peacocks.

Tearing meat
from bone of breast,

the warriors swallowed,
with the ale,

six feet of bronze
and iris-green,

blazing blue
turret of throats,

all-seeing eyes.
And it was no

dream—the old
servant

sweeping up
stinking rushes

after the feast
saw the evil eye

upon the floor,
skeletons

of war lords
in the open door.

ECLOGUE AND ELEGY

Before the ants,
before the crows,
before the old hunting dog,
I found the bird.

The black mask
stared upward from the
olive gray head.

The yellow breast
shone in the sun.
The sound of *witchery witchery*
in marshy land, in tall grass,
stilled.

From the clear memory
of what I saw,
I speak a universal word.

TUNING FORK

In the uncertain weather
of September
we planted a sugar maple.
By November

yellow or orange leaves
with key fruit
were gone. Now, two branches
buoyant and straight

mounted on our hollow earth
give out the tone,
constant in pitch.
Each, alone—

frieze of sleet,
ornamental snow,
halo of sunlight—
is original, new.

And the tuning fork
of young wood
vibrates Yahweh's:
It is good.

CRICKET ON THE HEARTH

I killed a cricket—it was leaf green,
large as surprise.

Struck down the buoyant leap, the music-making wings,
pale, thick body.

Scooped up his long horns, chippering good cheer
on a scrap of paper.

I've had my bad luck for today.

BEFORE SNOW

Here a portent broods
not dread, nor fear,
only the grey
turn of the year.
Through the gaunt trees
patrolling the west
uncertain clouds bar
a vast unrest.
The air broods soft
as a great cat's paw,
but the fur bodes cold
and stings like a claw.

Once the snow falls
there will be peace....
So the taut heart strains
before release.

CHRISTMAS

with a bowl of paperwhite narcissus

The cluster of flowers
follows an inner code
creating fragrant stars
taking position
in the galaxy of everyday.

So camel-tenders
and magi leaned back
on history
and the Persian sky
listening to a desert star
pull them toward
a Jewish child
with the face of God.

PORTENTS

Two o'clock:
a fanged wind
hurtles garbage cans;

deliberately,
a spectacular
cardinal

plucks scarlet
from leafless
branches.

I scrape
pigeon droppings
from the kitchen

window. Snow
is coming
whining like a dog.

At the Beginning

The first real snow came late, in March.
Through the night, updrafts of whiteness
billowed, settled, crusted, packed.
In the morning, small boys came

to this special place: behind old stables,
a hill of snow floating to a hockey field.
They had no sleds, trays, not even
cardboard. It'd been long

since they had snow. They raced the slope,
dolphin-poised, came down head first,
zippered windbreakers lunging into snow,
faces burning cold.

Intense, and caring,
they prophesied the moment
when, each in his hour,
would be taken by love.

SPRING SNOW ON LONG ISLAND

When my brother called
from Centerville
(ten minutes from Long Island Sound)
he skipped telephone amenities.
"We have mourning doves
nesting in the backyard maple tree."

"You had them before. Last summer?"

"We did. But this is March.
We're in a snow storm. I can't
believe it. The female warms
the flimsy nest. Snow comes down
like powdery cement.

I had to go to her. But
when I neared the tree, she flew up.
I saw—level with my eyes—two white eggs.

I backed into the house.
The mourning dove dropped to her nest.
Almost immediately, snow cloaked her.
She sat, unmoving. Snow outlined everything except that
    love song
coo coo I heard the male
singing weeks before."

"I can't believe it."

My brother stopped.
Wires sang silence.
I thought of Thomas, finger ready
to feel wet blood in Jesus' wound,
watching his dry finger in God's breath.

BIRD IN THE HAND

It must have been late dawn when the thrush curved his head
into the April air and incremental sunlight;
neophyte sheaths of song in the white breast,
the red-brown feather and wing bars spread;
touch of tree tops on the tail mumming the wind.

>He was still warm in the hand
>after the broken flight
>into the deluding freedom of the closed east window.
>He drowned in air at the impact,
>like a plummeting graph.
>Only the stain of feather on feather,
>the sharp calligraphy of stiffening claws
>for epitaph.

Bird in the hand? Rather two in bush,
three on branch, on bole; a flock in the glades;
the ponderous bequest of proverbs resigned to errata.

Whether restless wren hiving the privet hedge
or poor-grey mocking bird singing in the careful arcades
of thorn upon the lime,

or the foliation of the crimson head and breast
upon the half-decaying oak, the hammered sound
staccato on the headwind of the morning;
or the *kip, kip, kip,* from a cardinal mask,
or the iridescent grackle plucking worms from rain-pocked ground;

or the robin on the cherry tree—the cherry tree
like a toy, a varnished red and green
for posters for the Father of our Country—
the cherry tree where buttercups stand shouldering
the sunlight till the robins come and scatter sheen
of light to plunge of falling fruit
and scattered flight of robins in a dialect of spring;

even the crows—beaks still wet from plunder-flight;
or the brown and yellow back of the flicker,
or the sparrows never sold from creaturehood,
or the long *bob…white, bob…white*
from glittering grass in the swampy wood.

Here is a stunted heaven—bird in the hand.
One or many on bush or bole or bough,
rather than—feather on feather neatly folded
over the growing cold—bird in the hand now.

Where There Is No Rabbit

It is easy enough to remember how to make
rabbits with your fingers on the wall;
it is a harder thing, a harder thing,
not to recall.

As far as the road only this—
bent pins of grass, half lucent with ice,
the teeth of oak leaves ridged in sleet,
the disentanglement of splice
of weeds. This year there is no rabbit
glazed with cold, pushed against the wall,
lost and beaten, as the one we watched last year—
ears back, thighs tensed, fur shaken and tall.
Breath and life—little more than this he had;
except for the wind on his fur,
the silk chinchilla roughened up,
there was no move, no stir.

The dogs came, and we were awkward at his going,
sensing that the memory would habit
the undone good we must recall here in this place,
where there is no rabbit.

INSTRUCTIONS FOR THE PASSERSBY

There was, beside the air conditioner and
under the overhanging ledge, a hand's

breadth of stone window sill. Here
the pigeons made a nest: a sphere

of dry grass and weed, flimsy
as rhetoric, grotesquerie

of safe/secure. The male sat, a repose
of rock with a fixed eye, verbose

as stone. The female came at dusk,
nudging herself in place with a brusque

downsweep of wings, bosomy cluck.
Her eyes crowded us, like a truck

clearing the lane. So they sat, he
and she, for five weeks. And we

watched. Under them, two eggs, white
and glossy, warmed by day, by night.

The pigeons, hard as billiard balls,
held us with their look. Lightfalls,

dawnings, never early, never late,
they tamed us: how and why to wait.

Moss Garden

Saijo-zenji, Kyoto, Japan

Moss is what it is.
A drop of dew
and minuscule kingdoms

rise and send out
envoys of hope: to
forests and flowers,

fairy cups and cushions,
flowerless plants and fruit
on rock, tree,

damp earth
along a luminous pond,
beside a stream,

on bridges of log,
small stones.
Moss holds the rain.

Moss is what it is.
jade? emerald?
light shining from eons.

God takes flesh
this way
or that

shows himself
hiddenly
as here he is

impossibly possible
in this garden.
Moss holds the rain.

STRAWBERRY PATCH

These days are circumscribed with sun—
now cool, damp May is over,
and the fields are rich, sweet purple,
grown hand-high in hills of clover.
Here on the sandy sloping fields
sprawl rows and rows of berries
flushed to the same deep purple-red
of the orchard's ripened cherries.
Light and harmonious hums explore
the thick, low shrubs, and tiny things
dart out in small ecstatic leaps
on delicate translucent wings.

Then take the weary heart in Spring
to young farm hills of Thabor
and kneeling see God manifest,
and learn the dignity of labor.

THE WALLED GARDEN

A garden enclosed is my beloved...
Song of Songs

Not I. It was always He,
the garden enclosed.
That little I humanly knew
even in the early days
of—if not youth's ecstasy—
all singable ways.

And read the *Song of Songs*
again in raveling years;
aware of the poisonous fang
on the path; the briars;
the fountain noontime glistening
but quenching the fires.

This is the first time
I have been inside
a walled garden. Home
is what the heart was made
to have. Horizons, tame
as flagstones laid

in pathways, graze
on the moss of the wall.
In fuchsia bells, bees doze
and suck; while butterflies
petal the vines of sweet peas.
I listen with my eyes.

I do not stir. To be
listener and lover
is to forget to do.
O singer of Israel, this hour
a garden enclosed is my
beloved: the Word made flower.

From a Summer Diary

Only memory holds
that hummingbird,
too delicate

to be fossilized.
The female rubythroat
deposited her eggs

in a nest lined
with cushiony cobweb,
moss, fern fronds,

lichen, strands
of hair. Then I watched
78 wing beats

a second, less
than a penny
in weight.

Who lit
this wonder
for my eyes?

How can I speak
of God
except in the presence
of God?

SUMMER MORNING

Morning is no Moses,
wears no veil upon those
horns of light.

Past airy leaves
squirrels astronaut
in space;

white enamel
droppings shine
creaturely

of birds.
My own voice
cries silently,

echoing
from childhood
play:

Come out, come out,
wherever
you are.

And I
tremble
at a presence.

NUN IN A VICTORY GARDEN

Her wide exploring thumb is laid
upon the smooth tomato cull,
her big hands creep beneath the hum of sound,
there is no stir—a lull,
a breath—no more,
the mantis jerks his awkward legs along
just as before.
Her shabby shoes are courteous
of shoot and vine;
a martial line
of cornsilk
waves her on her way.
Within her steps a saucy squirrel spurts;
she picks a faded apple from the tree,
the squirrel stops and gnaws in ecstasy.
She wears a Poverello heart
beneath her old black habit,
and from her sleeve will someday peer
pink ears, then whiskers,
then a rabbit.
She lays upon the convent table,
harvest fruit still warm with sand,
that those tall boys
who lately planned
to tease her for her apples and her berries
may pilfer other harvests from her hand.

SUMMER

fills the white enamel bucket, overflows
its red rim with black-eyed susans.

Light has poured into
the brilliant petals hugging

purple-black, cone-shaped discs.
Hairy leaves, thick stems

gulp water in the bucket.
From a sunny meadow, I carry it

into the house pioneering backward:
decades ago, wagons from the west

loaded with hay and sweet clover
carried the seed of black-eyed susans

—the blessing on common things—from
Massachusetts to Georgia

so that Walt Whitman could say:
every hour of light and dark,

…every cubic inch of space
is a miracle.

ANY SUMMER AFTERNOON

My father was a wine importer—Pre-Volstead Act. In that day
etched decanters rang the intimate chimes of his marriage;
were still lifted—cautiously—for our christening rite.
He drank red wine of Chinon, I think, because Rabelais
was born there; he said the taste of truffles was in white
Pouilly-Fumé: the flower fruit was Beaujolais.

Prohibition quieted the dinner table talk. My father lapsed
into mockery. My aunt placed the glassware high
on a kitchen shelf. But whenever we children climbed near it,
we shined the hand blown flask, the cut glass miniature;
filled long necked decanters with sunlight. With dry
humor my father toasted the comic spirit.

Leave an almost land-locked harbor for France.
First the Loire valley, then the Gironde, and after
wet weather in Médoc, to pour bell sound and vintage
to the memory of my father.

DOG AT MY FEET

Is he asleep? dreaming?
on his back,
rear paw upraised,
eye-white cracking
through the half
drawn lids? Thin
belly heaving
out and in.

The paws tremble,
ears stiffen
at the death
to which he listens.

*Come back, come
back* I call.

And he returns—
with all
the terror
like bright flies
sticking to
his frightened eyes.

I cradle
his head,
brush from
his coat
fear that hangs
from his
churning throat.

Together we
return from far.
I also know
what such dreams are.

Common as Sparrows

He takes
the key

and shuffles
out to

look for
the mail.

Across the
door sill

the old
dog waits—

watching.
His eyes

speak: if
no love

should come
today,

love is
here.

END OF THE SEASON

My father used to take the boys to the sandlot
to practice curves; and Saturday afternoons
way up in the bleachers, they would shout
through a doubleheader. Home runs
the team made then, no one makes any more,
even though my father plans it for them
with the TV table pushed against his chair;
sunlight pouring whitely in his room.

Before an inning is over, the eyes close;
he wakens—startled—on a slide or foul,
and droops again. When his grandsons' cries
curve the dinner table like a careening ball,
my father smiles, approves the team,
and looks and listens like a trembling lover.
Gently his children watch this last game
of a season almost over.

IV

A REMEMBRANCE

of things past: John Berryman
slated to speak in the Mayo Auditorium
and almost every summer session student
vowing to be there.

Packed house: Berryman shuffles
past the lectern and stares.
Silence. He wants *more* of that:
absolute quiet. Absolute thickens
phlegm in dry throats, coughing rattles
the room, notebooks slide, a cigarette
lighter clinks against an arm rest,
breathing its fortissimo....

Absolute silence

After a long time he does not read his poems.
He talks about Anne Frank. He holds her diary
like a host, speaks of her presence.

Of that evening, I remember
three thoughts: "Anne," he said,
"disciplined herself to get up each morning
as though hope were at the door.
There has not been so witnessing a word
since Augustine's *Confessions*."

Grace is everywhere.

DREAM SONGS CONCLUDED

in memory of John Berryman 1914–1972

Henry was sick of winter, John dying of
living. Together they walked across the bridge

to the library. Following truth, no doubt,
John said. Truth detoured,

going home the short way—under water.
John followed like a bulging sack.

Henry turned,
fled back to the printed page.

Under black water truth cored the river.
John sucked the dark totality into his lungs.

Truth absorbed the pull of tide, plunged
into the root of water. John followed,

gained momentum in desire, felt the coldness
of the fire, brilliant burning of the root.

While sirens stopped to let the grappling
nets into the river, someone gave the story

to the press, the pictures to T.V.
"He chose the wrong way."

Not so John said not so. Mercy and truth
are one in the root of the river.

At last I am free.
I am free.

ISMENE

Antigone was the brighter
of the two of us.
A shrug-off person,
a little annoyed with fuss

and palace rules. She
was my father's favorite.
Not my mother's. Once
a seer had a fit, or perhaps

a vision at the shrine
in the inner court.
Everyone ran. My sister
stayed. She knew the report

they gave my father. She
touched my mother's jeweled pin.
When I could not look at the pulp
where his eyes had been

she said: you *must* look
and remember. Creon's son
never stopped looking
at her. Finally won

her for bride. That was
before my brother was fed
to ravens, and I sickened
at the overfed

glut of the vultures.
Antigone did not wait
in the cave; she
chose her fate.

Wailing clogs my ears
to this day;
the smell of funeral pyres
never blows away.

I, Ismene, am dead;
I am Creon's ward.
I have a little knife.
I have a cord.

I use neither.
I try. I fail.
Antigone lives forever.
And I tell her tale.

MEDEA MOURNS BRIEFLY FOR ORPHEUS

Orpheus had sung
the marriage hymn
at their wedding.

Jason listened
though his eyes
never left

the golden fleece.
Under ceremonial boughs
of the island,

Medea herself
had lidded
her eyes

to watch a
settlement of worms
at her sandal toe.

Nevertheless, she
wished now
that the Ciconean

women had not
torn Orpheus to
bleeding shreds

for his scorn of them.
If Orpheus were
alive, he might sing

now, before the nurse
brought Jason's children
to their mother.

If his hand
flamed the lyre
string, he might melt

that smooth round
stone that banged
in her breast

where Apollo's priest
said a human heart
was supposed to be.

VISIT WITH SAMUEL BECKETT

He drank the champagne
convivially, drank for the name
Lachrymae Christi—letting his fingers

taste the stenciled words
as the angle that he poured
stretched like a yawn. He went

to see his play—saying wrong,
all wrong. It should be sung,
it should be salt on the skull,

flame on the truncated edge
of a sword, should be the ridge
of mystery where poems stalk.

Listen to the bruise-colored years,
the penny-whistle noise. Look at the tears.
And silences.

The heart, that stubborn instrument
of love, promises only the blunt:
the word will have the last word.

NOT ENTIRELY ABOUT MIRACLES

for Flannery O'Connor

Even a man who asks for miracles
would wonder
how to live with one
when it came splitting the atom
of *known*.

Wedge a sliver of tomb rock
in a private reliquary
for conversation at the cocktail party?
sell the good news
before the ad men freeze it
into a cliché?
persuade (like Noah) a wife
that floods do come?
Even a man who asks for miracles
might wonder.

But this, that hardly anyone calls
a miracle:
telling the truth, now,
from this vantage place
where blood of redemption
spatters everything
and words cry
like those touched by the gods:

Listen. Listen.

Toward an Undefinitive Life of Flannery O'Connor

i

All writers are local somewhere....
Flannery O'Connor

Trace her lineage
to Adam, to Eve

in the garden.
Riddle what she gave,

what understated,
overloaded;

choices imposed,
or choices taken.

These storm the thin woods
of the world.

The smallest leaf is shaken.

ii

The key word is see....
Flannery O'Connor

When her father was young,
and she was a child,

she kept pea fowl
and a chicken that lumbered

like Gammer Gurton.
Later, they remembered

how little she said
while jeremiads slumbered

in her small bobbed head.

iii
The salt of the poem lives on....
Lawrence Durrell

Faulkner
she put aside

as one whose rhythms
would override

her plain tale:
the desperate

sacrament—man
conniving with

his own decay.
She read Conrad

and James
whose traces

would not diminish
the Mauriac faces
enduring her truth.

iv
Prophecy is a matter of seeing....
Flannery O'Connor

Honesty, dry
heat,

opened like
a parachute

in the enormous
shadow

of her crutches:
the comic

in the uncanny,
neurotic, demonic—

the human face
I look at

is me.

v
To be humble in the face of what is....
Flannery O'Connor

In the end   Old Adam
she heard the clear-   talked southern;

eyed devil   her brother death had
say: "Friend,   always been about,

you write *that* crap?"   sworn by God
Then she knew   to lift her out

Ezekiel's vision   the fiery jewel kiln.
totally true;

THREE FROM THOREAU

i

SONG OF THE WOOD THRUSH
"Whenever a man hears
it, he is young...."
He forgets his fears.
Whenever a man hears
it, he smiles; his tears
become lyrics to be sung.
"Whenever a man hears
it, he is young...."

ii

TWO WOOD THRUSHES FLEW INTO THE FORSYTHIA
When a wood thrush came this spring,
another followed: the song was true.
Yellow forsythia seemed to sing
when a wood thrush came this spring;
the bush was alive as a wedding ring:
one perfect song rounded from two.
When a wood thrush came this spring,
another followed. The song was true.

iii

TAKE THOREAU'S WORD FOR IT
"Whenever a man hears a thrush,
it is a new world," says Thoreau.
No matter the haste, the rush,
whenever a man hears a thrush,
spring comes with dogwood flush.
Someone said it who ought to know:
"Whenever a man hears a thrush,
it is a new world," says Thoreau.

NEW YORK: LOWER EAST SIDE

Sally Fitzgerald lectures on Flannery O'Connor

Outside the Catholic Worker
House on East Third,
the street quiets.
Panhandlers huddle
in stair wells, winos hunker
over heat grids, pushers
chart the alleys,
bag ladies rummage life
from lifeless matter.

Inside, to a Friday night
gathering, someone talks about
Flannery O'Connor
who never was
like anyone else.

Flannery did not misjudge
the ultimate resurrection
of the freak-prophet.
She knew grace triumphed
on the moon-crusted empire
of the devil; that,
terrified, man is free
to become more human.

Listeners pull toward
the speaker, sit hard
on wooden chairs, staring
beyond the dark windows
where grace pours down,
as always, violent.

How Tom Sawyer, etc.

The boy has a summer job:
on the muddy shore
of the library lagoon
he wields a seven foot pole
with a net (he is four
feet—standing high).

He sweeps the net
into think-scummed water:
salvaging beer cans, plastic
lotion bottles, McDonald's
cups, pizza platters. He bags
debris like Aeolus
keeping his winds.

Then the kids come with their dog.
They reconnoiter. Finally *Let
me Let me.* Ecstatic, the dog
slithers in mud, showering them all.

Thoughtfully, the boy hands over
the net. It is heavy. They recoil
from Newton's Law. Try again. Again.
The boy watches their arms ache,
pontificates—pack the trash
carefully.

Later, he sits above the silt
whistling an off-key tune
of the entrepreneur.

TRY IT ON

you said. And so I did.
Cleopatra's moss green
emerald with its beaten
silver galleries hid

the third of my finger bone.
I remember spaces of time:
Pliny's golden lion with an eye
of emerald; the talisman stone

of Charlemagne and the rose
of carven beryl that some say
Cortez brought back; how a
woman in childbirth knows

its potent healing, yet
the virgin wears it for
her purity. O I give
it back. Let it beget

upon your hand a mystic tree
of blessing on whose green
veined boughs birds sing
eternally.

for Katherine Anne Porter

A Christmas in Baltimore

When she was driven up Park Avenue,
to visit that old friend of Paris days,
F. Scott Fitzgerald was already drunk,
Scotty played carefully with the still-
ness of a rabbit, and Zelda, a strained
equilibrist, teetered on the rim of
everyday.

December 24, 1934—hemlocks in Druid
Hill bent, tipped with frost; miniatures
of gold nativities glowed in Walters'
Galleries, the smell of fruitcake, bread
and suckling pig, prodigal as light,
teased shoppers at the market stalls;
carols climbed ropes of miracles from
Peabody walls; under-the-tree-gardens
tenanted the homes on Biddle Street
and Charles.

Gertrude Stein, an overload of ambiguities,
with Alice Toklas, there to build them
into nouns and verbs, came to visit the
Fitzgeralds.

Scott sobered to her presence. Zelda
showed her paintings timidly, and rose
from the ruins of her heart, called by
honest praise. Their daughter clutched
a walnut shell signed by Gertrude
Stein.

F. Scott Fitzgerald saw his guests into their car. "Thank you," he said, "having you come into our house was like—as if Jesus Christ stopped here."

One day, Christmas, in Baltimore.

SPRINGTIDE

The twig that should have trembled
toward the canticle of water
lay untouched.

          Liberal, erudite,
the critics waited for the Welsh
fairytale morning to come to noon;
better, dusk. If the spume of white
water splintered the rock, fissured the sand,
pallid as milkglass, the witnessing moon
would reveal it.

          His underground river fanned
with sonorities drawn from the source.
Radiant perception molested the layers of stone.
Springtide and floodtide deluged the poet.
He drank: convivial and alone.

On rereading the early reviews of the poetry of Dylan Thomas

No Dirge for Dylan Thomas

There are four great elegies, I tell my students,
(and this no gloss on any one of them)
bell branch lamentations for the singer,
encumbered stars blown from a pastoral stem.

> God is patient with His poets,
> Eden-lonely, bruised to anger and surprise,
> aware of each historic leaf, and tavern-joy,
> the festering bat, the clamorous eyes.

> God's sun is blooming loudest now for Dylan Thomas,
> rage, rage, is coppery colored in a spire;
> the tumbledown tongue is prodigal home;
> light breaks from secret, dark desire.

There are four great elegies—it does not really matter.
And this is no dirge for singer, nor songs he never wrote.
Lament for song (I tell you this, my students)
that I should ever cause to dry within your throat.

IMAGIST AT CONEY ISLAND

One decade into the 20th century,
Pound, with his back

to Brooklyn, pointed his beard
to the Atlantic. Simply

to receive the kingdom, Ezra
linked arms with John Butler Yeats.

Their shoes filled with sand. Pleasure
rode the water, solid as Staten Island Ferry.

At dusk, lights rose like a fever chart,
Coney Island "marvelous against the night."

In the amusement park Yeats
rode an elephant on the merry-go-round,

"smiling Elijah in the beatific vision."
Pound leaned against a railing

pouring sand from each shoe,
words ripening in him in August heat.

Portrait of the Artist

The day we drove over the crowded bridge
that spans the Liffey, someone said,
"They make Guinness of this," an edge
on the smile. No one laughed. Dead

Joyce was alive and this was his
river. The whispering city repeated over
and over the words and phrases
he took from it once. Wherever

we went in Dublin, he had been there
before us. Odd, how the years' long rain
pounds on the streets but never clears
his shabby boot prints from the stone.

Professor of Medieval Balladry

Forty years he has pursued his love.
By dilettantes at once amazed, perplexed,
he peers beyond them, over, back again,
probing the footnote text.

Upon the minstrel his scholarship broods;
sluicing an intricacy of word, he stares
abstractedly around the graduate seminar
till everyone nods back, and smiles, and shares.

He reads the ballads like an unselfconscious lover.
Suddenly with a "hey, nonny, nonny," his feet,
huge and forgotten underneath the desk,
pick up the ballad beat.

Once long, long ago, fishing in the creek
between his toes he oozed the sun-streaked mud;
no less warmly now there curls between his toes
Robin's greenwood, Edward's blood.

FOR A CLASS IN SHAKESPEARE

Bordered between
grill work of sun and shade,
and the powdery black board
with chalk dust trayed;
the worn words of prayer
we use as grace;
the weighted-with-wonder
commonplace
of opening text
bookmarked with letter and note
pulse the morning,
a psalm in my throat.

Hamlet's inconclusive pain,
Falstaff's roar,
Desdemona's tears are on our lips,
dozens of times we have read it before,
it is always new.

The bell will ring,
take grief and joy
and bantering
from out our speech.
But the words are there
under your cap
of child-bright hair.

Never again shall we need to say:
"…and so—the play ends."
Forever, the book lies open
between us, friends.

NOTES FROM A TRAVEL DIARY

I had seen *Hamlet*, other places, other times,
and did not expect it there—
at Oxford. Now remembering, it seems
Christ Church Cloister gave me more
Shakespeare than Old Vic or museum tomes.

We sat on weathered church steps
looking at others often as at the play:
something like faith, perhaps it was hope,
shone in the willing eyes that saw
anguish and triumph on young Hamlet's lips.

Midland cold numbed me to the bone,
and still I watched and listened. The ghost
of Hamlet's father stood and spoke upon
the upper gallery. Then a single thrust
of wind blew a sparrow gently down

into his words. Even if I could forget
Hamlet's cloak brushing my shoulder as
he paced madly through the archway, yet
not this bird. Whatever Shakespeare chose
to share—was it less than life?   I wrote

only this: "Saw *Hamlet* today
at Christ Church, Oxford." But a bird
falling into my attention, a sparrow,
threads of feather, no song at all, declared
a prophecy in that old play.

Where creaturehood affirms itself—stirred
to proclaim diviner plan—there is my bird.

HOPE

When Prospero broke
his staff and drowned

his books, a nebula
of pearls crowned

his magic art
under the deep blue sea.

Pain becomes a poem
in the solitude of mystery.

Memory in tidepools
of the mind

rearranges sand, domed
shells outlined

in rainbow.
The holdfast

of seaweed feathers
the rock, and lasts.

SATURDAY AFTERNOON AT THE WRITERS' COLONY

Benignly, a member of the Board
of Trustees came to bless
the writers. He could afford

the luxury of patronage
now—after the stockyard
years. He bent the hedge

of privet quietly hoping to find
a poet like a Keatsian pearl
in the center of a sand-grind

of words. He found—sleeping
near the sunlit stream—the poet
naked as a piece of string.

LISTENING TO THE COMMENTARY

on the death of Ernest Hemingway
July 2, 1962

i
He was cleaning a gun.
There was no note. He wouldn't care
what they reported. Who can say.
No one was there.

He was a Catholic. Not
any more. When does a man
stop being what he is. He
was a Byron. No, a Mark Twain.

The thing to do is last
and get your work done, he said.
The Sheriff gave the coroner
time for his report. Dead?

ii
Generations not yet born will refute
that word applied to him. He chose
his own order of people to love.
In India, Australia, China, everyone knows

he had the Nobel Prize for
the Old Man. He was free and brave.
And the President mourned.
Burial. It will be like Joyce's grave

a—The picture magazines did well.
He was a drinker, fighter. But now,
after the tempest. Now.
He, too, plucked the golden bough.

Thomas Jefferson at Seventy

Crippled wrists and fingers make
my writing slow.... And yet

I have a mockingbird I often take
from out its swinging cage. A pet?

I think of it as something more.
The strong feet grip my flesh:

down-curved, the bill explores
my hand. Gardeners bring fresh

seed for me. And then he sings.
That repertoire! My whole life—

a golden age of seeking—rings
in his galaxy of song. Pain? Strife?

Yes. But hope has steered my bark.
Men ride their fear in skiff or ark.

I take a mockingbird into my dark.

OBITUARY NOTE: LILLIAN HELLMAN 1905–1984

The Times gave her an obit page: "Miss Hellman
left no survivors." Other facts: dates:

birth, death, plays, early, late.
Dashiell Hammett; the Fifth Amendment;

An Unfinished Woman, etc. etc.
And I…for half my lifetime, have watched

years runneling down her face;
listened to her draining search

for truth: trenchant, prophetic,
compassionate. I have left her theatre

resurrected from the world's sorrow
for a moment, holding fish and honey-

comb in my hand. Say what you will,
facts lie. She has survivors.

THE LIBRARY: SOUTH STAIR

Never use the elevator.
Choose the south stair—up or down.
The heavy door swings behind you
and you are in Poe's Dupin-dusk
climbing past the pock-marked cinder blocks—
each a coffin wide and long.

Walk slowly;
a sorcerer's light, pale mustard yellow
seeps from a narrow skylight.
Hercule Poirot may appear,
head bent a little left,
waxed moustache pointing upward.

Lean over the stairwell, breathe
the air Perry Mason once exhaled
in courtroom oratory.
There is a scarlet wheel
that will unleash a waterfall
should Peter Wimsey command.

Always, before research or scholarship,
walk the south stair.
Detectives clear frustration, guilt,
confusion. Fixed laws
control the universe, and
once you find your carrel in the stacks,
Jane Marple will appear
with a cup of tea.

AFTER THE EL GRECO EXHIBIT

They were exhilarated with the elegant
sobriety of Spanish dons; tapering
hands and elongated heads;

saints and Mary poised like
leaping fires of salmon, opaline-
pink, cinnamon, blue-green of

juniper berries caracoling on
a rock horizon. At a stop light
on the parkway, someone glanced

at a suburban lawn. Flirting with
the fading light, a goldfinch—
like a rabbit from a silken hat—

rose to the topmost branch
of a sycamore, flight feathers
overlapping filaments, downy

feathers air-trapping song.
This other gift.

THE COAT OF FEATHERS

The son of the emperor
Hsuan Tsung, wore, over his armor,
a sleeveless coat of feathers.
Across his breastbone, the tremor

of body plumage of the drake;
dark glow of copper pheasant
on his shoulder, and like overhanging
tiles on his back, renascent

green barbs and webs (also from
the pheasant). Striding the palace
in his sleeveless jimbaari, the emperor's
son felt his immortality. Yet Patroclus

having only Homer's song about his
armor lived longer; the son
of Daedelus continues
his flight to the sun. A twine

of hemp covered with feathers
in the Oriental Room, British Museum
seems to be all that remains of
the prince. Enough for a slight poem.

One drop changes the ocean's deep.

DALI'S SACRAMENT OF THE LAST SUPPER

Children stomp around the gallery watching
the electronic receivers rock
against their polo shirts. Downstairs, someone
is giving a lecture on Dali and Braque.

Dubious listeners study the wall: "The
Sacrament of the Last Supper" and turn
gratefully to morning haze—light as dreaming—
in Monet, or to Pissarro's fields that burn

under the Gallic sun. In this room
of visions, communing angels, arc and line,
twelve men kneel around crisp bread broken
and a curious drinking glass of wine.

No one looks for a presence—museum guards,
visitors, children—no one asks to be blessed.
But the old boats of the Galilean lake
move gently into His translucent breast.

V

AUTOBIOGRAPHY

Let my life go—in the will of God—this way.
Let it affirm the impossible
for the impossible is evident everywhere.
Little can be proven absolute from day to day.
But there are: faith, love, prayer—
indomitable frailties that phoenix
before and while and after I say
Amen.

INITIATE THE HEART

Consider the season's wheel:
the turn of summer creeping over
leaves one incurved tendril on the vine,
one pointed peak of sweet, late clover.

Initiate the heart to change
for it is wiser so,
accepting the splendor of the hour
white with clematis or snow.

Fortify the will with peace;
no season taking root,
tranquil in mist, in warmth, in frost,
each bears fruit.

COME CHRISTMAS

They waited for the city bus
the rabbi and the nun;
he was so old, he must have known
his son's son's youngest son.
She and her companion were
description-proof as far as dress,
one thought of Canterbury Tales
and Chaucer's prioress.

The bus was crowded and the rabbi stood,
jostled and awkward on his tired feet;
she took his hand and paid his fare,
and helped him find a seat.
He murmured some old blessing
and she bent down her head
as one who knows the value of
the swift prayer surely said.

There was a stir within the car,
and man to man was not a stranger,
seeing Isaiah prophesy,
and a virgin stand at her own heart's manger.

Do Not Keep the Letters

Do not keep the letters
that she wrote;
her loyal love will not be held
within the margins of a note.
Whatever she has written
has known its own travail,
to nurse the peace and pain now
is no avail.

Sooner find a star
to wax and press,
than prison in your box
her loveliness.
Spring goes,
and with it violets.
Having knelt at purple springs,
no man forgets.

AFTER SILENCE

Down the mountainside
cool spray of glacier water
falls into the meadows of wild flowers.

From this faraway place, you send
love's improvident gift:
wild blue flax, yellow

cone flower, stiff-petalled
Indian blanket seeds. Disbelieving,
I sift them into moist soil.

Today, in the live universe
of a flower pot, silken leaves
spear upward: a fragment

of the day of creation.
The gift is so much the giver.
I bend to the frail green

like an amateur trying
to photograph butterflies
drinking from a stream.

Veronica's Veil

It was in the summer kitchen
that I first noticed it.
The stone floor had been hosed,

was wet-cold in August heat.
For hours we had sat peeling
peaches to preserve. Sticky

juice bonded my fingers;
bees followed thick trails
of syrup down my arms

from the silk-suede peaches
carrying orchard sun and rain
into my hands. A long time ago.

But I stare at my palm right
now. When I dropped that
paring knife to stretch and

unlock stiff fingers, there
was an image in my palm.
Whose? Who made peaches—

flesh clinging to flesh
like memory? That human
face creates me, too.

NOTE ON EXODUS

When their feet crack frost underfoot,
each of the nuns
breathes a plume of cloud
truer than a weather vane
moving before her.

In early winter dusk,
when they return from the inner city,
hospital, school—
Venus, a lover's knot of fire,
drops from branch to branch
on leaded trees,
leading them into the horizon.

But one night (no cloud, no fire)
I kneel in a narrow room
listening to the clatter of a throat full of stops.
One of us is nearing the promised land.

I echo with my sisters, "Mercy, mercy,"
while a priest bends over her
touching with oil
the dark canyons of her senses.

How different from that print
in my childhood Bible:
Joshua's men trumpeting hosannas into Canaan,

and the followers shouldering grape vines
so heavy with harvest,
they dragged the earth like a king's robe.

THE LISTENER

I am listening. And I hear
    every human person calling me.
My whole self is in my ear.
    I answer totally.

I am listening. If I fear
    the pain of answering, the stress—
my whole self gathers in my ear;
    I answer—gravely—yes.

I am listening. What I hear
    is God creating me.
I concentrate within my ear
    that I may be.

I am listening. I disappear
    in God. Return. Live.
I trust that voice within my ear.
    I answer. *Let me give.*

ON REREADING AUGUSTINE

Who had sung the song
he did not know: *tolle lege*
take and read...*take*....
Life crowded Augustine:
wildness, sex, passionate
needs, festering pears.

Leaves stirred, a bird sang
on the garden wall: *take*
and read...the sing-song
of a child. Augustine wept,
picked up Paul's letter
and read: Make Christ
your armor.

Who had sung that song?
Who sings to you? to me?
Before I dare to say
I do not know, I hear, once more,
the many-voiced bird
singing in the cage
of my reality.

THE WORD I LEARNED

The word I learned to rhyme with *breath*
was *now-and-at-the-hour-of-our-death.*
Death, the word, did not seem odd
taught by a Sister—wed to God—
the word I could not understand,
like *apple, Christmas, book* and *hand.*
When grandpa was not in his chair
with lullabies and jumbled prayer,
and I was free from school to go
and watch his coffin down through snow,
breath I could touch in rise and fall,
the other word they said was a *call.*
Then *breath* was the distance from sleep to waking,
the other the hurt in my pulse-beat quaking:
the distance spanned, what I had seen
from the "Visitors" door to the hospital screen.
The word I used to rhyme with *breath*
is love of my Father, is unshaken feather
held to the lips; unspoken word on parted lips;
is blessed wax clinging to cold finger tips.
What it means I do not know,
but hour by hour I quietly go
to the word where Mother is, and grandpa, and friend,
where song has neither beginning nor end.
For need of a rhyme with the lovely word *breath*
nothing is better than loosing the tether
and running like hope or like thought
from the things they are teaching to the exquisite TAUGHT,
saying over and over with every breath
now-and-at-the-hour-of-our-death.

BE YOUR TEARS WET?
—King Lear

*A decomposed body, believed to be that of a missing Catholic nun,
was found in a trash dump. Death was ruled as homicide.* UPI

i
Carols of snowbirds
winter over the dump ditch

and her decomposing body
with its secrets. This is

my body, too, that saw
his eyes, knew the destiny

of terror. Her name
is mine, sister, and

that same altar where
water fountained from the

heart turning to blood
in words of vowing.

Can these bones live? broken
under metal knuckles?

From stench and anguished
taking—radiant grace

rise virginal to sing
Piccarda's song? *His will*

our peace? while spirits
move like snowbirds

in the blinding mystery
of light?

ii
Can these bones live? or
shall we make reed baskets

in the desert? or bake
our bread in dung again?

can these bones live? or
shall we stagger forward

like crippled flies on
heating pipes? can these

bones live? or shall we
dull our quick desire to clot

like suet cooling on a
plate? shall these bones live?

iii
It is God's voice that is
continual surprise, unchimerical,

plain as pain. Not Kafka's book
an ice-ax breaking frozen seas

inside, but unrhetorical I AM.
These bones live. Frail and

certain as the shadow of a
butterfly.

MESSAGE FROM INLAND

I am clothed
in the seamless
garment
of fog.

No gulls cry.
No nervous horn
sounds
another ship.

No fragrance
of kelp stirs,
no wind
of sea-change.

Red mud slips
like a secret
beneath
my feet.

I know
what happens
to seamless
garments.

I have lashed
a riding
light
to my heart.

A Second Praise of Loneliness

I took my well-bred theories
and patterned them in praise,
I said—this is the way that I shall meet
my lonely days.
I knew I would be proud to go
tearless and strong....

I did not know that dusk is bleak
and stripped of song.
Step by step probed hollowness,
infinities of space
black as velvet, soft and weak,
pressed on my face.
God of loneliness, I prayed—
there was no prayer—
my tired eyes reached out to find
the altars stripped and bare.

Now with my brave words tightly furled,
in silence and afraid,
come, O my Love, I ask in the night,
come to the wound You have made.

WAITING

I walk through silence.
A Red Sea parts straight
before me, closes again
over the chariots of sound.
I wait.

On red mud, I walk
unpracticed, unadept. Late
in learning, my heart is a Miro
bell, one side without a shell.
I wait.

I tell myself: be ready
to be unready. Sate
yourself with nothing; want
nothing more than that.
And wait.

I am a climber up far
enough to see air vibrate
beneath me rather than
above. I only know enough to
know: wait.

HERE ONCE THE WILD ARBUTUS GREW

The Sisters' Cemetery

Here once the wild arbutus grew; pink-hoar,
white-frost, moist-cool.   The students walked that way
to skirt the woods; they knew if it were May
the shell-frail buds would break with fragrance for
the spring, this was the better part of lore
to learn.   With quick, young hands they came to weigh
a silken collar with a fragile spray,
or twist bright petals in a pompadour.

Where once arbutus grew, the nuns are laid
like quiet prayers.   Hands folded on the breast,
they face the towers that their hopes assayed
of crucifix and vows together pressed.
So students find—one hour, one breath apart—
a spray of wild arbutus at the heart.

Suggestion for a Nun's Obituary

Be brief with eulogistic speech,
recording blueprints of her labor;
cautious of the gospel of her calvaries,
the foothills of her Thabor.

In her no radiance could be seen:
ember and ash, but rarely fire.
Write this: God loved her, and
greatly she desired to desire.